DAY LAUNCH FORMULA

HOW TO CREATE AND LAUNCH THE
ULTIMATE NICHE PRODUCT TODAY SO
YOU ARE MAKING MONEY BY TOMORROW

Bryan Westra

Indirect Knowledge Limited
MURRAY, KENTUCKY

Bryan Westra/Indirect Knowledge Limited
2317 University Station
Murray, Kentucky/42071
www.indirectknowledge.com

Book Layout ©2014 IndirectKnowledge.com

Ordering Information:
Quantity sales. Special discounts are available on quantity purchases by corporations, associations, and others. For details, contact the "Special Sales Department" at the address above.

Day Launch Formula/ Bryan Westra. —1st ed.
ISBN-10: 0990513246
ISBN-13: 978-0-9905132-4-7

Contents

Contents

Dedication to Jennifer Bonilla

Our income is often – and by often I mean almost always – directly proportional to the amount of goodwill that we have with our marketplace.

—FRANK KERN

Welcome to My World!

H i and welcome to Day Launch Formula. My name is Bryan Westra, and I've been doing day launches for as long as I can remember now, and perhaps that's says I don't have the best memory in the world, or it's just that I've done so many that it seems like I've done them forever. But, the truth is, I have done tons of day launches and I've learned a few things along the way, which I will be sharing with you in this course.

Let's get started by just asking ourselves why we might want to do a day launch?

A day launch is literally a mini launch that you do within the confines of a single day. So that's a rather basic definition of what a day launch is, but let me make it a little more specific for you...A day launch is a launch that you do within a matter of 5 to 8 hours of a single day. The reason you do launch them within a 5 to 8 hour period, and certainly less when you get really good at doing them, is simply because you want to be able to enjoy your life, don't you?

Some of the reasons why you want to be able to do a day launch is to enjoy your life to the fullest, but what is really the main reason most people want to be able to do a day launch? Well, I think it's pretty obvious but I'll just go ahead and spell it out: people want to be able to do a day launch because of the money. There is an incredible amount of money that can be earned doing day launches—if done right. Every time you do a day launch, you exponentially increase your opportunities for earning income on the Internet.

Now, I'm sort of a crazy individual in that I'm an extremist. I do everything in extreme measures, so that I can get extreme results; namely, results that most people can't get. And so for that reason I would refer that you check out our disclaimer as far as income is concerned, which is located at the front of this book. So let me just begin by saying that your income is in no way guaranteed. I don't think you can possibly know exactly how much money you will make doing a day launch. So, for this reason, I can't really predict what your results will be, as most of my results vary from launch to launch. What I can tell you, however, is that these launches are a lot of fun; require only a little bit of your time; and can make you money if done right—at least that's my opinion.

So I mentioned the word fun…

Fun is one my favorite words, simply because it's short, sweet, and expresses exactly what it means. Fun is one of those expressions that can be very specific; yet, on the other hand, be very abstract. When you are having fun in my opinion you are engaging in play. In other words whatever it is you're doing is not considered work. In my opinion work, is more or less the opposite of fun, and so for that reason I don't like to do anything that is considered work, because it detracts from me having fun. And, I think a lot of this has to do with mindset.

What some people find fun, other people consider work. It's sort of like the same old adage that one person's garbage, is another person's treasure. Now, I don't know exactly who came up with that, per se; but I bet the person was a junk collector... Ha ha!

On a more serious note though, let's really think in terms of what we're doing when we're doing a day launch: so let's turn our attention over now to what is a day launch, shall we?

What is a day launch?

A day launch is something you do day in and day out to generate money. More specifically its product creation in the form of information that is digitally architected. That sounds almost a little technical, and it really shouldn't be, because very simply a day launch is you getting together with a good friend, and having a normal conversation with them, teaching them something that you just learned about, that you're excited about in the moment (that you might not be excited about later), and something that you want to get them excited about also. Because, let's face it—excitement is contagious—and it's also a state in which people buy things.

I got this idea of doing day launches from an old habit that I had acquired in between studying for classes in college. I would call up a good friend of mine, who incidentally was a college dropout, and together he and I would meet for coffee at a local coffee house. The coffee was pretty expensive, but the conversations, I guess you could say, were worth it.

He and I would rattle on for hours after hours after hours, until nearly the coffee shop was ready to close down for the night. I would miss a lot of class time getting caught up in these conversations.

No no... I know what you're thinking...

And the answer's "No. I didn't drop out of college," and in fact I graduated with a 4.0.

There was something very valuable in the conversations that he and I would share. He was a science geek, and he liked to go on the Internet and watch all of these videos on YouTube about new improvements in science and scientific breakthroughs, and all these sorts of things.

Me on the other hand, I was more along the lines of Internet marketing, or finding out ways of making things simplified, or even I used to talk a lot about writing classes I were in, and different classes that I had, and some of the things of the professors in class would lecture on.

I love to study, in fact; I love to learn new things. I think that was something that my mother must've instilled in me at an early age, because she was an avid reader, and she used to take us to the bookstores, all over the country (my father was a truck driver and so we traveled a lot) and she would buy us all these books on various topics; basically anything that interested us she would buy us.

So, one day I had my tape recorder with me; the one I used to use for recording lectures in class, and it just so happened that I started recording the conversation that me and my friend were having unbeknownst to me.

When I got home later that evening I found that the recorder battery was dead, and so I figured that I must have had left it on accidentally. What I learned was that the recorder actually had recorded the conversation my friend and I had that afternoon on the recorder. So what I did was actually go back and listen to the recording of me and my friend talking.

I then took that audio and developed it into a short course, since the topic matter was very interesting, almost 'podcast like' — sort of like the podcast interviews that many people are doing nowadays. Incidentally you could actually apply this same approach (podcasting interviews) to this formula I'll be teaching laying out for you in this book, to possibly make your day launch even richer, but I'll let you come up with this type of idea on your own, as I simply want to get the basics down for you in this book, so that you understand the formula that you need to follow in order to be successful with this Day Launch Formula.

So, to make a long story short, I sold a few copies of this 'out of the blue' training I put together, which actually happened only to be a conversation between two friends sitting in a coffee shop.

The ironic thing was is the money that I made off from selling those audios that formed the course: they more than paid for two years' worth of that expensive coffee at that expensive coffee house. So that was cool. I had residual coffee income to allow me to do more of what I enjoyed, at that time.

Anyway, I do want to teach you a little bit more about exactly what a day launch is. We've already sort of hinted at what a day launch is, but to spell it out for you in layman's terms: A day launch is literally going to consist of you getting some tools together in order first be able to do a day launch, then, you picking a niche (and this can really be anything that you're interested in or anything really that captures your attention, but something that you don't mind talking about hours on end). I know everybody has one of these interests, though some of us may have to dig a little deeper in order to find it inside ourselves, than others will. The next thing basically includes doing some basic research, so that when you talk to others about what it in you already know you have a little bit more of a grounded basis from which to express yourself. So this basic research is going to open you up to sounding a little bit more, shall we say, 'expert-sounding' at what it is you already know. And then after doing all of this you're basically going to follow the formula that have laid out for you in this book and then wake up tomorrow and do it all over again, and then wake up the next day and do it all over again—again. And you're simply going to repeat this process Monday through Friday as often as you like (weekends too if you like). So the launches are basically the development of a single product that you will be having fun creating, and marketing on the Internet. You'll be doing this for the purpose of producing profits for you over and over and over again; creating what I like to call 'residual assets'.

A residual asset is residual income that you get on an ongoing basis through a tiny investment up front of your time and a little bit of your money.

Now I said a *little bit of money*, and that's exactly what I mean—you don't need to spend a lot of money to get your product created, but in order to sell it correctly you must be willing to spend a *little bit of money*, because you're going to need to come up with ways of branding your product so other people want to actually purchase it. This is sort of along the lines of 'you can't judge a book by its cover'; yet, everybody does in reality judge a book by its cover. If this weren't the case major publishing houses wouldn't spend thousands upon thousands of dollars on the design work for their book covers. They know that in order to get someone to buy their book they first have to attract their buyer's attention—and this sometimes can be expensive for them to do. And so for that reason you will need to spend *a little bit of money*, unless of course you have the skill set to do amazing product covers yourself. However, the downside to doing it yourself is also going to be that you're running out of time, and so you might think it best to spend a *little bit of money* having a freelancer to do the work for you; since come tomorrow you'll be doing the exact same thing all over again. We'll talk more about this later. For now, I want to turn our attention over to how else you can benefit from day launches, and my Day Launch Formula.

Okay, so, now that you have your product, and you have your marketing in place, and you have your various distribution channels (I will be sharing this with you of course later in the book) now it's time to set it and forget it. Basically what you've just done is you have created a product, marketed it, put it out there on the World Wide Web for everybody and their mother, brother, uncle, and fourth cousin to buy, and certainly everyone else as well, but now it's time to forget it. This simply means that you can't dwell on one product, and the success of that one product, because there is always a tomorrow. And, 'this tomorrow' is actually when you will be developing a brand-new product, completely separate from the product you developed the day before. So, you really don't have time to reflect too much on your work, as you're actually continuing to launch product after product after product after product, day in and day out. So when we get into understanding how else this can benefit you, it may sound as though you're doing something for nothing, but on the contrary; what you're actually doing is creating so many residual assets, in such a short period of time, that you start dominating various niche markets with your products, while creating wealth for yourself in the process.

Dominating a particular market can have its just rewards: You can start to have other people want to market and sell your products as well. When this happens you make even more money, indirectly. You also become branded as an expert in many different fields. And, with that branding of being an *expert*, you also become the go to person whenever someone has a question, or needs an answer, or someone to spin ideas off of. These types of relationships can be very beneficial, especially when it comes to doing future day launches.

But, for most people at the end of the day the primary benefits of doing a day launch are simply: (a) making a lot more money, (b) working a lot fewer hours, and (c) being able to work out of the comfort of your own home, doing something you absolutely love, and that you would never in a million years call work—because everything you're doing is fun as all get out!

So I just wanted to cover in this short introduction some of the benefits and the structure behind exactly what a day launch is. Also to give you some insights intuitively you can digest a little more easily this book, before we actually get into the Day Launch Formula.

There is a lot of content to cover in this book, and so what I've done is chunked it down into various chapters, some of which have subheadings that make it easier for you to reference, as well as digest, and remember. The main purpose of all of this is of course for you to be able to implement the Day Launch Formula immediately, straight out of the box.

For many of you, reading this book, some of these ideas are going to seem a bit strange, for some of you they are going to seem extremely radical, for some of you they won't resonate and you will probably want to through this book away, and for others of you, you'll find yourself in a category of individuals that are highly driven and motivated to make an incredible amount of money doing something they fabulously and absolutely love; that is, so that you can enjoy the type of lifestyle you've always dreamed of. That last category is actually who I'm looking for, in terms of the market in which I'm selling this book. The people that find this book utterly repelling, I recommend you give it time, because the ideas actually do begin to grow on you after a little while. The reason that I know these four type of characteristics in terms of how people usually feel about the Day Launch Formula is because I've actually beta tested the system on several different personality types, in both people inside of our marketplace as well as outside of our market. The reason I did that is because I wanted to be able to discern how people thought of my product who were inside of our marketplace, but I also wanted to be able to understand people who were outside of our marketplace and what they thought of our product so I could get some ideas and advice and insights into how I might build or improve on the Day Launch Formula to make it even better for those inside of this marketplace who might be kind of on the fence about the whole Day Launch Formula deal.

So just rest assured that you're in good hands, and that very shortly you can be working, or I should be telling you that you're going to be having the most amount of FUN you probably ever had in your life; doing something ultra-creative, and super awesome, and something that by the end of the day you will be able to pat yourself on the back for having completed something that is just spectacular, and something that will perhaps bring you great rewards, and definitely help you fill your bank account a little bit

XVIII • BRYAN WESTRA

easier. And another great benefit to the Day Launch Formula, before I forget, is simply learning a lot more things about things that interest you. And I think there's a lot of value in that aspect alone.

On that final note I just want to explain to you that as a child I used to read all these books on many different topics. It could be that I was studying art and drawing in one breath and then in the next moment I was studying piano lessons and karate, but I was always an interested learner. This means I was always doing something that was engaging my mind and my curiosities about other things—things that I had no idea about. Because of this, I used to hate when people would tell me, "You need to focus on what's important here... Pay attention to your education and your studies... And forget about all those daydreams and things that will never bring you any real lasting success." I think by the time you implement the Day Launch Formula, you'll find that I proved them wrong—I can make a lot of money in my daydreams.

To Your Lasting Success!!

Bryan Westra

CHAPTER 1

What You Need

'm not going to waste any time here. The following items are must for this to work. Of course I do realize many of you reading this book will likely have tools and resources as well as skills and competencies that will make this process even easier than I explain. Keep in mind, I am writing this book for the person with little to no experience in internet marketing, much less someone who had ever done a launch before. Even so, if you've done launches before, have a world of knowledge and skills, and think you know what you are doing, I know you will find immense value in this system, because there's not one remotely like it that I can tell.

The first thing you're going to need is a YouTube.com account. Once you signup, assuming you don't already have a YouTube channel, will be to create a channel video introducing your viewers to a niche that you're going to be promoting yourself as an expert in. The reason for this isn't why you think: The reason is because the next thing you're going to do is monetize your channel with Google AdSense. To do this you will need an AdSense account, which you can get by going here: adsense.google.com. Once there you will find some instructions for setting up an AdSense account. Before you do this, however, monetize through YouTube first, by clicking on the 'monetize video' link which can be found somewhere in the back of your YouTube dashboard. Chances are this link will take you to adsense.google.com, which will make the process easier for you. If you get confused, just visit YouTube and type in the search 'how to monetize a YouTube video with AdSense, and you will find resources to help you set this up.

What you need to know about YouTube is that you can make money with it in a variety of ways. These include:

Affiliate marketing: This is where you do product reviews on YouTube.com of products you like and endorse, and place affiliate links in the video description area. When viewers click on the link, and buy the product, you get a commission for referring the sale.

Commercials: This is where you sell commercial advertising spots on your own videos. This will require that you have a strong viewership, and that you know how to sell ads to corporations, small businesses, and online sellers. When your YouTube channel has a ton of videos on it, and you've got a lot of subscribers, then you'll be in a better position for negotiating commercial ad space on your videos.

Marketing: This involves marketing your own products and services. You can link back to your blog, a lead capture page, or give away a free e-book to create value in you and your brand to encourage more viewers to subscribe to your channel (making it more valuable), and to connect with your niche market more one-on-one though the comments section. You can also link back to your Facebook, Blog, Twitter, and other social media sites. This a powerful way to engage your viewers and convert them into customers, while increasing the life time value of your customers.

Sponsorships: After your channel takes off and you've got over a hundred thousand subscribers, and videos with well over a hundred thousand to over a million views you can call on companies to pay you to sponsor their products. Companies do this all the time with the major motion picture houses. You might see James Bond driving a BMW and drinking a Pepsi. BMW and Pepsi Cola pay to have their brands associated with movies people watch. It's great advertising for them, and because they're mass marketed companies, it is a great way to market their brands on a mass scale.

Product Development Platform: Google Hangouts can now be recorded and automatically hosted on your

YouTube channel. So if you do a Hangout in which you teach something useful to those you're on the Hangout with, letting the Hangout be recorded and placed on YouTube.com, what you can do after it's uploaded is download the video with software you can purchase, and then take the video down off YouTube, so that you can sell the video as a course, for profit.

There are a lot of other creative things you can do with YouTube to make money for yourself. I really like this platform, and creating a short video, less than four minutes, gives you opportunity to sell a product or service as if you were right there in front of your prospective customer, and connect with them in a more authentic and meaningful way. You simply need to turn on your thinking cap and you'll discover many, many, ways to make money with YouTube.

The next thing you need to do is setup a Skype account. You can do this, assuming you don't already have one, by visiting www.skype.com. Skype is a voice of internet service provider, which allows you to communicate both verbally and visually with anyone else who has a Skype account, for free. You can also message people using Skype, as well as send files back and forth to one another.

You'll essentially be downloading some software onto your computer, which will let you know when other people, in your Skype contact directory, are online. You can set your status to available, not available, off line, busy, etc.

etc. etc. so you don't have to worry about people contacting you when you're busy doing other things online.

The next think you will need to do is purchase a Skype Plugin that will allow you to record both the audio and video components when you're 'Skyping' with someone else. The plugin I use personally, which I find very useful is SuperTinTin which can be purchased at: www.supertintin.com. This plugin has six different options for recording:

None. Neither of the video streams will be recorded, only audio.

Picture-in-Picture. Both of the video streams are recorded, with the one that you viewed during the call exactly as you saw it, with the video of yourself inset within the other video.

Side-by-Side. Again, both of the video streams are recorded, with each of the videos occupying half of the screen.

Local Only. Only the video that was recorded (of you) by your web camera will be recorded.

Remote Only. Only the video that you viewed during the video call will be recorded.

Two Files. Both of the video streams will be recorded separately, into two completely different files. TIP: This is useful if you use the two videos for completely different purposes.

We'll be using Skype and SuperTinTin (or your other plugin of choice for recording audio and video on Skype) for developing content for our product launches later on in this book.

The next item you need to possess or have a subscription to is, Adobe's Premier Pro. If you don't own this already, you can purchase for a little bit of money this software by visiting Adobe.com and subscribing to this software. Premier Pro is a world class video editing software. If you own a Mac, you may prefer to use another video editing software. It doesn't matter which software you own, it really only matters that you have the capabilities of editing your Skype videos, as hiring a freelancer to do this can be costly, time consuming, and they may not render the quality you need to properly launch your product. If you have never used Premier Pro, you can get a lot of instructional tutorials free by searching on YouTube.com. If you haven't guessed, I love YouTube.com. I believe a person can learn about anything they need to for anything to do with business or their profession simply by taking a trip to YouTube.com and doing a video search.

The next thing you're going to need, and perhaps this is a no-brainer, but you'll need a laptop computer with a web-cam and microphone. This is to communicate with someone through Skype. There are other technologies that would perhaps work better than these, but you'll need this in order to use SuperTinTIn and have both your side of the video, as well as the person you're engaged in conversation with recorded into a synchronized video file.

You will also need an articulate and willing friend to chat with for extended periods of time on Skype. This will be a definite requirement, and you should plan on spending at least two hours with this person on Skype; talking in one hour intervals. It would be ideal to have someone who can chat you up with a blank or neutral background behind them. You really don't want someone who is sitting in their bedroom with clothes and posters tacked up behind them on the wall. You want to keep the focus of your audience, and the best way to ensure this is to have them (and yourself) chat with a plain white wall behind them, and to have them communicating with you in a nice quiet area, where they won't be disturbed. You definitely don't want a noisy child wining in the background, or a dog barking at a mail person. You get the point.

The next thing you will need is a Fiverr.com account. You can set this up in a matter of moments. It isn't difficult. What Fiverr.com is, it's an online platform where people provide freelance services and products for just $5 per 'gig'. A gig can consist of a lot of things. For our purposes you'll be using it for having audios transcribed, e-book covers designed, and the editing of your transcripts done. You might also use it for other services that you find more challenging or less desirable with this whole system; though, I have designed this system so nearly anybody could follow the steps, and successfully launch a high-quality product in a single day.

The next thing you will need is a website/blog. You can get these free through www.blogger.com or my preference www.wordpress.com. If you are technically inclined, or have the funds to hire somebody to set one up for you, I highly recommend setting up a self-hosted WordPress blog. You can do this through most c-Panels, or simply by going to www.wordpress.org. A solution, if you'd like to attempt to set this up, might be to go to YouTube.com and watch a few videos where other people explain how to set this up for you. The purpose of having a website is many-fold: You want to self-promote and brand yourself and product lines. You also want to integrate all of your online marketing efforts through a central hub, which Word-Press is fabulous for letting you do. You can also host sales pages and thank-you pages as well, which will let you sell your launch products, without having to go through a third-party subscription site like leadpages.net. If you don't want to set up a website/blog, then you'll definitely need the next requirement, though I recommend you have this anyway, regardless if you already have a website/blog.

The next thing you'll need is a www.leadpages.net account. This is a great outlet for creating low-cost, highly effective, sales letters and thank-you pages. This outlet also provides analytics, which is basically statistics that let you measure how many people are visiting your sales pages, and how well your pages are converting into sales. Leadpages.net also integrates with major auto-responder services like Aweber.com, GetRespons.com, and so on; to capture traffic and sales leads, for future follow-up campaigns. Having one of these accounts also lets you do A/B split-testing to determine how well your copy is performing, so you can make adjustments as needed. As an online marketer you need to be able to measure statistically your advertising, so you learn and predict what your return on investment is for any given launch.

Next you'll need to set-up a Click Bank account. You can do this for free simply by visiting: www.clickbank.com. Click Bank is the world's largest information product affiliate marketplace. Here you'll be able to sell your information products using the power of affiliate marketer's promoting your products. You'll also be able to use Click Bank as a means for selling your digital launches.

Next you'll need an Amazon S3 account. You can set this up, and if you've never set one up before you'll be able to (as of the time I'm writing this) use this service for free for one year. This account lets you host videos, and other large files for very little money. You'll be able to host your entire launches through the Amazon S3 server, and the servers are very reliable and never down. You can set up this account by visiting: http://aws.amazon.com.

After you've set all these accounts up, you'll have all the resources you'll need for creating quick launches, that can be created in a day, and ready to sell by the following day. Throughout the rest of this book I'll be laying out the strategies and instructions on how to implement day launches, and later explaining how this will set you free financially, and have your income constantly and consistently increasing day-by-day, week-by-week, month-by-month, year-by-year, and so on.

CHAPTER 2

Pick A Niche

A niche is a subsection of a market. For example if you want to sell animal products, you may want to niche down to selling dog products, or you may want to niche down further and stick to dog training products. The key is not to niche down so small that you have a limited market of potential buyers; however, you do not want to niche up so high that you get lost in the competition. You want to find a fine medium where you can stand-out in a market, and compete without all the noise and clutter coming in from everybody else selling to that market.

There are many ways of finding a niche that you can sell to, however, generally speaking, you want to stick to a subject at first that you are passionate about. Studies have found that if you create a product around some topic that you already know, and are passionate about, you'll be more likely to 'stick' with it, and have better follow-through. I cannot underscore this enough.

I am a hypnotist by profession. I specialize in particularly sales hypnosis, indirect hypnosis, and hypnotic language. These are the areas of the profession that most resonate with me and which I find most interesting. For this reason, I have written books, taught classes, and developed other training aids around this niche. Other people in my niche are interested in 'pick-up artist' and 'stage hypnosis' as well as other areas that fall into the hypnosis and NLP marketplace. These less interest me, and so I stick with what I like best.

I suggest that you find an area of expertise that you are familiar and passionate about to begin with. Then once you have exploited these niches with your product launches, you may want to learn about other areas that are also profitable and which you can create launches for.

If you still are saying to yourself, "I don't have any interests or any ideas for a niche," then I would suggest taking a minute to stop reading this book and reflect on you day to day life. What is it you do? What are the activities that you involve yourself in? Ask yourself questions like, "If I could do anything, what would it be?" Then start generating some ideas.

If you still feel stuck, I recommend visiting Amazon.com and perusing some of the books over there. Take note of the types of books which interest you. Look at the covers of the books, read the titles, and discover what excites you. This may be an area you want to start with, first, and later you can branch off into other areas as you become more cognizant of what peaks your interest, etc.

More ideas, which I have found useful involve visiting YouTube.com and checking out some video tutorials. There're a lot of neat things to learn and discover on YouTube. I mentioned it back in chapter one how I have used YouTube to learn many things business related. YouTube actually helped me complete my MBA and graduate with a 4.00 GPA. Had it not been for this incredible resource I wouldn't know half as much as what I do now. There are a lot of really cool ideas common everyday ordinary people like you and I share up on YouTube. It's not only entertaining, it is also highly educational and a great way to kill a boring day.

Another thing I like to do for inspiration is to visit local bookstores. I can lose a lot of hours in a bookstore, because I love to read and investigate what other people have to say in words. There are tech magazines with the latest gadgets and upcoming products, there are magazines on financials and investing, there are books on personal and professional development, there are books on New Age and Metaphysical subjects. There are also books on: eastern religion, philosophy, business, computer programming, travel, animals, and you name it. One thing I like to do is shop for some great books and inch my way over to the in-store coffeehouse to drink a great tasting gourmet coffee, while I sit and read the books I've picked up. I also find that there's always people willing and wanting to engage in conversation at the coffeehouse section of these bookstores. Sometimes I get inspiration and insights simply from talking with other people, perfect strangers, that help me to understand something, or who give me their two-cents. I don't think there's anything wrong with getting somebody else's point of view or even stealing their insights and repurposing them into your day launch products. The whole idea of a day launch is to take free information and turn it into a product people are willing to pay for and get extreme value from.

In life you go through a lot of 'changing' circumstances. You're constantly being spun into different directions and experiences. For this reason, I think having an idea journal is a fantastic way to come up with ideas for launches (and I do this myself). What I do is have a smartphone with a forward facing camera, in which I have downloaded the EverNote app. This app syncs with my other devices, so when I'm on my laptop writing, I can pull up those ideas without having to pull out my smartphone. The cool thing is I have the ability to snap photos, record ideas audibly, and even write on my smartphone with a stylus notes and ideas to myself, and do this all through the EverNote app. A lot of these 'raw' notes and pictures have made their way into books I've written much later on. It doesn't matter what your preferred process is, the main thing is that you have a means of collecting ideas and insights as they pop into your head. If you have that stellar idea, but you don't immediately write it down, I can almost guarantee you'll forget the idea, and likely also forget that you even had the idea in the first place. Having an idea journal, you'll one day have an idea, write it down, and sometime later (not a long period of time later) be looking through that idea journal and discover an old idea and you'll be glad you had it written down.

At my desk, I'm always taking sticky-notes, for formatting book cover dimensions, telephone numbers, email addresses, and so on. At the end of work day (I work from home doing this full-time) I gather up all my notes and take a picture of them with my smartphone and add them into my EverNote notebook designated for 'random sticky-notes'. I cannot tell you how many times I've needed something a day later, only to find it waiting for me back there in my EverNote account. I love EverNote.

Believe it or not, inspiration is all around you. You're constantly getting ideas, seeing things happen around you, taking a mental note of something somebody said, that you start jostling around in your head when you're walking away from the person, and there are millions of profitable topics to create products around. If you don't believe me, just visit Amazon.com and take a look at any of their four million and climbing books published each and every year. There is always an abundance of ideas, you just need to find the right one, which resonates with you, and commit to developing a 'day product' around.

CHAPTER 3

Basic Quick Research

n this chapter we'll be looking at the research necessary to create a 'day product launch' to where you deliver the ultimate value to the consumer buying it. The types of products you'll be creating must teach something to your buyer that they don't know. If people already know, what it is you'll be teaching them, they'll not only be bored, but utterly upset they wasted their money on your product (not to mention their valuable time). I cannot tell you how many Amazon reviews I've read where the reviewer made comments similar to, This stuff is newbie material, nothing of any real value! You don't want to be this type of producer; instead, you want to create content and fashion it in a way that is completely unique, exciting, and which inspires motivation in the buyer to take action.

I compare this to the metaphor of what I call, 'The Boring Teacher'. In my high school, we had two teachers that taught Honors English Literature. The subject matter being taught was exactly the same. The problem was, some of the students hated learning, while others loved learning the material. The students who hated learning the material were those students who happened to unfortunately get placed in the 'boring teacher's' classroom, while those who loved the material were fortunate enough to be placed in the 'awesome teacher's' classroom. It was the same material, same lesson plans; however, one teacher made learning fun and exciting, while the other was there for nothing more than a paycheck.

The number one thing to remember when creating your day launch product is to make learning the material exciting. I want you to take a moment and visit YouTube.com and search for video on something that interests you. Make sure there's more than one video covering this topic. Then I want you to watch two different videos, by two different channel owners. Chances are one of the videos is more interesting and fascinating than the other one. One you connect with more, and find more valuable intrinsically. The other, maybe you dislike it, or not, but you'll think less of it, as you have something better to compare it to.

In sales, and this is important for you to know, there are oftentimes two unique products that are essentially the same. You have a generic version, and a name brand version. People will more often buy the name brand product, over the generic product, even though it might cost three times more in price. Why do you think this is?...

I earned my MBA in Marketing. I studied exactly why this is, which was explained to me as the name brand product has greater name recognition, people feel more closer to the name brand, because it has a promise that it is consistently known for delivering on, and because they intrinsically somehow, for whatever reason, have bought into this idea hypnotically that the name brand product has more intrinsic value over the generic product. People love brands. People will often times become so attached to a particular brand that they will defend it to the death, if need be (figuratively speaking of course). But, I have done a lot of research and I also concluded that one reason people love branded items more is because of the way the brand is presented to them. It goes back to the 'boring teacher' metaphor. People love exciting people, and the energy they achieve from associating with these high-energy brands is addictive. Logic may play a part in the decision to like a brand/content, but emotions make buying and loving a product hypnotic, to say the least. People want to be transported to new and exciting places. They want to be 'moved' and so more than anything else I can teach you, I must get across to you this point, because you MUST develop your day launch product with all of this in mind. You must move minds with your product, and then you'll move sales. This is the golden rule of selling and marketing anything.

Let's turn away from that core principle for a moment and get into the research aspects, because this is what you need as the foundation for developing any product. Remember, the information was the same for the two teachers; it was how it was presented that made all the difference in the world. First, we need the material, then we can work on innovating it to something beyond special. We'll get there, so tread with me for a few more moments, while I give you the run-down on how to research.

Why Research Is Important

There are a lot of great sales messages out there in the form of sales letters, video presentations, webinar presentations, and so on; namely, of which are utterly compelling, and which captivate attention, provoke interest, cause desire, and lead people to act and make buying decisions. This is the old sales message formula in fact: Attention, Interest, Desire, and Action (AIDA). This is all great an dandy; however, there's a problem with selling products that are well marketed, which capitalize on consumer behavior psychologies, and influence and persuasion principles. That problem is many products are developed after their marketing has been done.

Basically, here's how it goes: The marketing team gets together and starts to look for problems they want to solve in a particular marketplace. Then they get feedback from their market to determine what the market wants. Then they start coming up with some ideas. Then they develop marketing materials. Then they develop their product based on their marketing materials. The reason they do this is simple: They don't want to get sued for misrepresenting their product through their advertising. It is also incredibly easier to develop a product around the marketing, than marketing around the product. In sales, many sales professionals take a bit of a different approach: They learn (usually from the marketing materials, which happen to have been converted into sales presentations and product training materials by the marketing department) about the product's unique attributes, then learn about how those attributes convert into advantages for the consumer. These are logical selling points; that is, logical selling point for the consumer to be able to make a logical buying decision. Next, they look at how those logical advantages lead to certain benefits. The benefits are not logical; rather, they are the emotional results and attainments that improve the mental state of the potential consumer.

Let's really examine this for a moment: Let's take the example of someone developing a day launch product meant to help people work from home successfully. Let's pretend like this product really exists, and that the main feature of the product is that it only requires the buyer to write a blog post each day, and press a 'publish' button.

Nothing more, as the product is hosted on a parent sight that takes care of all the traffic coming into the consumers post, which is setup to sell affiliate offers on autopilot. Some advantage that immediately come to mind is that it allows the buyer to work, let's approximate conservatively one hour per day; leaving the rest of the day for them to do whatever. Wow this sounds like a really great sales proposition already, does it not? If you only were to present the product in this much light you'd probably still get a lot of sales of said product. However, most people (in my opinion and experience) make buying decisions based on how they feel emotionally. So what's left out of this equation are the personal benefits of that primary advantage. What are the benefits you ask? The immediate benefits that come to mind are: (a) by working from home only one hour per day the consumer can spend more quality time with your children so you can actually feel good about being a parent, and never feel guilty having to pay to have someone else raise them, (b) by working less you can experience life more on your terms and experience more joy and happiness in your life, and (c) by working from independently for yourself you can experience less fear and concern about how you're going to be able to pay the bills. So the benefits relate to specifically emotions like: feeling good, joy, happiness, and less guilt. These emotions are the catalyst for triggering a buying decision. This is what people deeply want through their values, and emotions that they don't want are eradicated.

If we know this, we know well what we need to present in our sales messages, but we have to be careful: With the products you will be launching each and every day, you must truly solve these problems and provide these benefits—not just sell an empty promise.

I'm serious! You must give people extreme value (a ton more than they ever expect), and more importantly you must follow through on the promises you make. The more value you provide, the more money you will make as a result. Ironically, if you only follow the money, you'll never realize it; yet, if you follow value, you'll receive more money indirectly than you ever expected to receive. You'll also receive proportional value back in the form of accolades and love from your buyers. There's something to be said about this. So please keep all this in mind.

To set the stage for all of this to happen, the first thing we have to do is gather research. The way we do this is to very quickly visit YouTube.com, Wikipedia.com, and http://scholar.google.com. Granted you can most definitely do other research on other sites as well, but I'll just keep it simple for you and list these here.

YouTube is an amazing place to do research, and I'll tell you why! You see most people that post a YouTube video haven't posted the information elsewhere, though they may have gotten it elsewhere. So the research is completely unique and already well researched generally. This means you're capitalizing in a sense on research someone else has done and now you're simply taking some notes on what they're presenting to you. It is a lot like being in a college lecture hall, taking notes on what a professor is lecturing to you about. The instructions are usually exactly what you need, because people speaking and presenting on video must get their message across in the most natural way possible. You can't do a YouTube video and expect to keep people's interest if you speak in a boring monotone or use language that only people in academia can understand. For this reason, this is one of my favorite places to do basic quick research.

Wikipedia is a great site for doing research also. The people who post information collaboratively on Wikipedia tend to keep the facts straight, and will criticize collaborators who do not properly cite their fact sources. I like to think of Wikipedia as the Cliff's Notes of everything. You can find a summarization of just about anything you want on Wikipedia, which usually consists of the history of what you're researching, the factors the caused the developments of what you're researching, and it gives you scope to draw certain conclusions based on the knowledge you already have. The best part is, and I love this, most all Wikipedia articles have references, and many of them contain links back to the original source. So what you can do is look something up on Wikipedia, and if necessary go directly back to the research that's already been done for you and compiled as references on Wikipedia. Easy and quick approach to doing more in depth research.

Google Scholar is an academic search engine that gives you quick access to academic journals and more scholarly research. These can be used for cases studies, as well as for expounding on. People love to learn something new; especially, when it is cutting-edge advancements in areas that peak their interests.

Remember, and keep in mind, the research doesn't have to be a long drawn out process. It needs to be quick and succinct only. Take shorthand, or do what I do: I compile my research altogether without really going through it too deeply, by clipping it into my EverNote account. Once it is nicely compiled there I can access it as I'm developing the information product. You can also share links to the research with the person you'll be teaching to give them some prior insight into what you'll be covering with them on the video call (more about that shortly!).

What you'll want to first do is come up with a strategy for how to present your product. This strategy must keep stay congruent with the idea I've given you about making the content later be presented in the way the 'amazing' teacher would deliver her content. It must also be unique and not-so-common. This means looking for ways to make connections with the research out there by determining how it plays out in solving the needs and greed of the buyers who will be purchasing it. You can do this mentally in your head, and take notes as you go, and later present those excitedly to your buyer like the 'amazing' teacher would have done to her students.

Research usually isn't necessarily exciting on its own. How it's presented is what makes it exciting. For now, just concentrate on finding an angle that will be further developed as you start creating the product. I'll teach you how to do this in a bit, no worries!

CHAPTER 4

The Day Launch Formula Blueprint

U p till now, I've kept you pretty in the dark with the whole Day Launch Formula. The reason I've done this is because now we get into the fun part. If you've already found a niche, and done your basic research, and formulated some brainstorm ideas about how the research connects to the values, needs, and greed that your buyer will be seeking out, then now you're ready to start learning the actual formula for success. But, don't get too excited yet, as there's plenty more to come—especially when we get into the number crunching much later in this book.

Essentially, the Day Launch Formula is a fifteen step process. You've already done some of the fifteen steps already. You're making headway, even though you don't know it yet.

Fifteen Steps

Step 1: Set up all your accounts.

Step 2: Do some quick research online regarding your niche. Take notes using EverNote.com

Step 3: Setup a Skype Video Chat with friend, and record both parties using SuperTinTin. Teach your friend, as though you were doing a private client coaching/training on what it is you're passionate about. Get your friend to play along as though they were the person who was paying you big bucks to teach them. Teach them for a minimum of two hours. After each hour, end the video call, and then create a new video when done.

Step 4: Use Adobe Premier Pro to edit the video. Add an Intro and Outro purchased from Fiverr.com for $5 each.

Step 5: Have the videos transcribed through Fiverr.com (cost is approximately $5 per every 10 min. of audio). So, approximately $30 per video ($60 total).

Step 6: Have a Kindle e-book cover created on Fiverr.com for $5. Make sure it is of the highest quality possible. You'll need to come up with a title, subtitle (make sure it solves a problem, need, or greed), and author name (Your own or a pen name).

Step 7: Have the transcript edited on Fiverr.com or do it yourself. If you do it yourself you can use Grammarly.com or WhiteSmoke.com.

Step 8: Take the transcript and turn them into a Kindle e-book, and list them on http://kdp.amazon.com.

Step 9: Take the formatted e-book file and video file and host them on a private membership site, Sellfy.com, eJunkie.com, or anywhere else you like.

Step 10: Create a sales and thank you page using Lead-Pages.net. On the thank you page give access to the hosted product files.

Step 11: Add the product to clickbank.com to sell through their affiliate marketplace.

Step 12: Create a YouTube.com Video to promote your new launch product. Make the video four min. or less. Add a link to the video description. Set-up a Google Ad-Sense account on your YouTube.com channel, and monetize the video by allowing Google to place ads on the video.

Step 13: Advertise and Sell the Product

Step 14: Call it a day

Step 15: Repeat this process tomorrow, and every day thereafter.

In the next chapter I'll be taking you deeper through this blueprint, providing you with some instruction and advice along each part of the journey. I'll be filling in some details to bring more clarity to your mind. For now, just familiarize yourself with the blueprint. This is more to give you an abstract broader view of the process we'll be going through today.

The reason this is an effective system is because it's an actual system. There are many, what I like to call: Mom and Pop internet marketers out there online today. This probably makes up 90+ percent of everyone selling online. The Day Launch Formula is the McDonald's of internet marketing, because everything is very systematic. You don't have to guess what comes next. You do certain things in a certain way and achieve a certain consistent result. These steps are like a check-off list, and you just tick each step off your list, each day, as you go through the formula.

At first, especially when you do this the first go-round, you'll probably experience a little dissonance; simply, because a lot of this (probably most of this) will be completely new to you. It will likely take you much longer the first time, especially given you have to setup all your accounts, and become familiar with how each platform and software works. The good news is this system gets easier and easier each time you repeat it, which hopefully will be every day. In time you'll be able to walk through these steps like clockwork, and so quickly you'll second guess yourself as to whether you followed the system correctly or not. In this way, this Day Launch Formula has the tendency to make the impossible—possible. People who have beta-tested this formula have reported back that they couldn't believe how possible it is to launch a new product each and every day. The main feedback, and most positive, incidentally, has been that people are amazed by how many streams of passive residual income they are able to bring in with this system. I love getting those emails from people telling me they thought they made 'x' amount of money, only to discover they made more than that through channels they had forgotten about. That's pretty cool.

Now, I'm one of the hardest working people I know. My father was a hard worker, dedicated to his job, and providing for his family. He didn't retire until he was in his late 70s, and he was a truck-driver—a guy who drove a huge rig with a 53' box trailer, all over the United States. He drove more miles in a year, than I will likely ever drive

in my entire life. That's dedication! I want you to understand that this system does require some effort on your
part. You have to work hard, to work fast. And, the faster
you work, the faster you get done each day, and the sooner
you can go on to the other important aspects of your life.
Don't make this system harder than it has to be. Learn it.
Acquire good habits with it. Over time it becomes like
breathing; you won't know when you're doing it, and it
will happen, and you'll be done, and each month you'll
thank yourself. By the way, I don't make any financial
claims about this product, and give no guarantees. I don't
know you. I don't know what you're made of. How possibly could I know if you'd make money with my system or
not! I also don't take any credit for your successes, either.
Those belong to you.

CHAPTER 5

Detailed Instructions

've given you the blueprint, now I want to walk you through each step, giving you advice and some of my opinions. You're welcome, of course, to disagree or to find an approach that makes more sense to you. I'm not here to hinder you, I'm here to help. I'm the good-guy! So let's proceed, shall we?

The first step is to set up all your accounts. I shared what accounts you needed in Chapter 1. I think what I would do, looking back on the first time I implemented the Day Product Formula, is take a full day to set up all the accounts. I wouldn't do anything else except take a few hours to set all of them up. I would also recommend that you store all your user names and passwords for logging in to the accounts in a secure password protected folder on your computer, where you can have them available whenever you forget your passwords. This will save you a lot of headaches in the long run. The frustration that can happen when you get locked out of an account, because you've not entered the right password after so many chances can be a nightmare. It can also set you back a day, and that's never a good thing, is it? So my advice is to set up these accounts, save the login details somewhere safe, and then take the rest of the day to do whatever.

The next day, after getting a good night's sleep, I would start with your first day launch. The first thing you want to do is find the niche you want to create a product for. Don't take a lot of time, there will be plenty of other days to create launches for other niches you might be interested in. Just pick one, and run.

After you have your niche picked up, immediately jump on the bandwagon and start your basic research. As you research usually some ideas and associations will start to come to you mentally. Take these insights and write them down, or record them in EverNote. They will be instrumental value points that you will make in your product, soon. What I typically do is start with YouTube and find some videos other people have made around that niche. What I find, and I think you'll find true too, is often times when people create a YouTube video tutorial, they will say something valuable that they don't even realize they're saying. For this reason, I try and be very focused on what they're telling me through the video. After watching a couple four minute videos, I usually have a general idea of the niche I'm operating within. I also pay particular attention to when the person in the video gets excited about something they're relaying. This could be a point, an idea, or anything really. These I usually assume to be important and valuable to the niche market. So I write these points down (record them in EverNote).

Next I move on to Wikipedia. There is usually some terminology in the videos I watch which are niche specific. For example, in the hypnosis niche, 'embedded commands' is a term that is commonly understood; however, outside of the industry it is less known. Wikipedia is usually a great resource for defining and getting an idea about what these terms mean and how they should be used contextually. Using the right terminology and in the right context when you develop your product is important, as it gives the illusion or image that you're an authority. I do recommend, however, that when you do your first day product that you create a product inside a niche that is already familiar to you. This will make the journey more pleasurable, and realistically easier. The first day of school should be easy, without any homework to take home.

After getting some Wikipedia information summarized and noted in EverNote (hint: you can web clip webpages into EverNote for easy reference later) I move onto Google Scholar. I like to find one or two scholarly articles, written by academics (if possible), as I know these people are likely to be reputed and well-respected in the niche. I like to cite them in my product launches, because name dropping people of importance and who are well respected gives the illusion you are well-informed about the subject matter. Also, it gives you opportunity to make your product more valuable in the eyes of the marketplace.

This is how I usually conduct my research for these day product launches. It's not really hard, and the more you do it, day-in and day-out the easier it becomes for you. Give it a chance to get easier and you'll be glad you adopted this system, I assure you.

Now I want to give you some insight into my process. I think you'll appreciate this, because I know I always like when people give me their opinions and insights about something they know more about than I do; especially when it's a topic I'm really interested in.

So I like to find anomalies. These are irregularities that are incongruent with how things are 90% of the time. I'll give you an example. For years people have spouted off about how people tend to be either 'left brained' or 'right brained'. Left brain people are said to use the left-hemisphere of their brains more dominantly. These left-brain thinkers tend to be more logical. They are good at learning foreign languages, and tend to excel in the maths. They like logic and reason, and it is beautiful to them. Then you have people who are right brained who are more creative, outside the box thinkers, where abstract ideas and emotions resonate more. These have been written about in books, cited by psychologists and famous people, and the media. Now some scientists are advocating that people shouldn't be lumped into these two classifications, as they are telling us that the real truth of the matter is people use all of their brains. At certain times, for various reasons people use certain parts of the brain more than other parts, but at no time does a person not use all of their brain. I saw a video on this a few days ago, and thought, "Wow! That's an anomaly, inconsistent with what I've always been taught about the brain. Something like this thought provoking, don't you think? It causes people to want to find out more details about it. These types of anomalies are great interest triggers. So I like to look for them and use them whenever I can in my product launches.

I also like to find the common thread that runs through the research. This common thread is usually the essence of the niche. If you can find a common problem, especially one where most people experience it, but for whatever reason have just accepted it as 'the way it is' and can find a solution to this problem, then you have a problem that people will identify almost immediately with when you talk about how you've found an amazing solution to keep the problem from being a problem. Ears will perk up, and many people will buy just for this reason alone.

I also like to find inventive ways to improve a process and make it easier. This is my natural propensity, and I've always, as long as I can remember back, have done this intuitively. This is actually the foundation that systems are created. I'm always, in my mind, trying to improve a process. This is one reason I was attracted to the field of Organizational Behavior in college. I liked dealing with process improvement plans, and helping companies improve on their processes to make more money, have happier employees, and lessen their costs. So look for the ways you can make an existing system better.

With this Day Launch Formula I wanted to create a system that would solve the problem of people not creating residual income streams for themselves fast enough. The bigger impact you can make, and the sooner you can roll out residual assets all over the web, the better your chances of making a huge sum of money. I mean that makes sense to me anyhow. I also don't like affiliate marketing, because everybody does that. My personal opinion is that prospects are stale to these methods. They receive far too many messages in their inboxes, most of which get ignored. As an online marketer you want to rise above the noise in the marketplace and get your product well-received by potential buyers. Everywhere you look there's an advertisement for something. There are so many, I think consumers are blind to most offers. It's sort of like there are so many things in our face all day long, we simply tune them out. Too bad for those companies spending billions of dollars on advertising getting less and less return on investment on their paid advertising dollars. Sucks to be them...or does it? They still make money, so I guess they're still coming up on top. I have always like the idea of having my own products for sale that other people couldn't sell, even if they wanted to! This creates scarcity, and influence principle, and it works...people buy products at higher prices because they know there's only one place to buy it, if they want it. Then the only thing you have to do is 'make' them ***want it***.

Next we move on to Skyping with SuperTinTin. This is an incredibly fun part of the Day Launch Formula. Reason being, it is when you actually get started developing a high-class product, easily. What you do is simply get in touch with a friend, or someone willing, and tell them you want to practice teaching a new class you're going to be teaching, and were wondering if they'd mind you teaching them one-on-one via Skype. You then add in, "I'll teach you for free, but I need to record our tape and record our conversation if that's okay, because you will, if everything goes smooth-sailing, be using it in a possible product launch you'll be creating." Most people, will ask you question about what it is you'll be teaching them, etc. You simply be truthful, and they'll let you know one way or the other. It's really best, and I always try to do this personally, but I like to find people who are already actively involved in the niche I'm developing a product for. I find people on Facebook groups, or through meetup.com. Most of these folks are more than willing to let you teach them something they're already passionate about for free. This is beneficial to you as well, because they often times add to the teaching, adding in their own two-cents and experience. This is awesome, especially if you don't yourself know much about the niche you're teaching about. Also, to be completely transparent here: This is the reason why only basic research is needed, because more often than not the real teacher is the passionate student you're 'allegedly' teaching. So they're actually helping you create your product, and free of charge. This builds in a lot of credibility and value in you and your product.

What you do when you're setting up to teach them via Skype, is make sure that they are in a quiet setting where they will not be interrupted by any outside distractions. I also insist that my guinea pig student has a solid colored curtain behind them, where their camera won't pick up any of the room. I ideally, like for just them to be in the cameral. This is important because you want your buyers to perceive this product as having high value, and, well, let's just be honest—if you have their open sock drawer in the backdrop, that's a bit off putting, and makes your product appear generic. You want to be a name brand product, not a generic product. Your customer expects quality and value—it's your job to provide it.

Tips on Product Development

I want to take a 'time-out' for just a moment and give you some tips and insights on marketing and creating your product.

Number one: Treat your 'product' as if it were a person—you love—even 'in' love with. If you are in love with a person you'll do just about anything for him or her. You'll do things for this person you might not do for anybody else. The LOVE blinds you, and you'll even start to see this person as a 'god' or 'goddess' giving them credit they don't really deserve in the eyes of others.

This person (your product) has charisma, a distinct character, and they are beyond any other quality—trustworthy.

Everyone wants to 'secretly' be this person; however can't, so they settle on the next best thing: they associate themselves with this person whenever they get the chance. They even go out of their way to make association with this person. This person is the next best thing to God. Everyone dreams about this person, and they won't admit it to anyone, but it's apparent to everyone who knows them that they are completely in love with the person, and want nothing more in life than to be with the person, in a relationship. It may be more than love; it may be obsession.

Your product must be the 'popular' kid in high school. The person everyone wants to be, but can't so they settle on associating with this person as much as they can. They take this person's abuses, and demands, and pay a heavy price for being able to be in the same room with this person, let alone stand next to them in the lunch room line. This is the person you want to be, to the extent you even offer them your lunch tray, and go without eating. You'll fast for them, because to you they are godlike. You want to be in favor with them. You also know that they don't need you; however, you need them. This is what you want people thinking about your product. Your job is to make this happen. How you do this is through branding. Branding is the facade you create around your product. It's the image. Your product's brand is created through the following steps:

I. List the most common attributes that your product possess. Attributes are a synonym for features, which are the aspects of your product, and what it does (functions). For example, let's say you want to list the attributes of a can of Coke. The attributes are spherical design, aluminum, twelve fluid ounces, pop-top tab, red and white design, caramel colored, sweetened, fizz beverage. These are the attributes, which describe a can of Coke. They represent 'what' the product is and consists of.

II. For the top attributes, list the advantages of each of those attributes. For example, going back to our Coke example, let's just take one (though you'd do this for all of them), let's take the caramel colored beverage aspect of the product. The liquid is caramel colored making it distinct, the taste is consistently always the same (even after all these years), and the fizz causes your mouth to tingle, when you drink it.

III. For each advantage, decipher the benefit of the advantage. For example, the consistent taste, makes the beverage resonate with me as a 'traditional' product. I associate Coke with my childhood, and the fun childhood memories on those hot summer days. In fact, if you think about it the same consistent red and white color scheme is consistent as well, and so is the color, and so is the twelve fluid ounces, and aluminum can. You might say that Coke is 'classic' mightn't you?

IV. Next decipher in your mind the common theme that runs through the product. I've sort of given this away, by hinting at the word 'classic', as we all know that Coke brands itself as "Coca-Cola Classic".

V. Next associate this common thread with human values. A value are the things people find important and believe in, and are deeply attached to. When I think of Coke, and it being a classic brand, I think of my childhood, and how drinking a Coke was a tradition passed up by my parents. I value my parents, and my awesome childhood, so these connect with me on a deeply emotional and value oriented way. I think if Coke stopped existing I'd be traumatized, and almost feel like I would if a family member died. Coke has a fairly strong brand, wouldn't you agree. By the way, I can't tell you honestly the last time I personally had a Coke, but I still love the brand, and what it represents. The longer Coke is around the stronger its brand seems to be, so long as the Coke tradition is passed on from one generation to the next, and people continue to value their connection to 'family' and 'hot summer days'.

Now you basically have your brand. This is exactly what you'll do with your own product. Then you position your product to your marketplace in harmony and congruity to that brand promise. Incidentally, Coke's brand promise is to bring happiness and enjoyment to people's life. A brand promise is where the marketer and owner of the brand has a vision of what the brand must be and do for the consumers. You must satisfy this promise for the consumer to 'trust' your brand, and in order to bring it to name brand status. It should be unconsciously identifiable, and it should be able to trigger an emotional response, while at the same time hypnotizing the buyer. There's meaning in the brand, when people identify with it and say they love it, without exactly knowing why they do. You do, however, know why people love your product, and it's not important that the consumer know. The popular kid is popular, though the geeks who idolize the popular kid don't always know why they idolize him or her—they just do, because the popular kid is a name brand; that is, everybody loves him or her, whether they know why or not!

You want his for your product. You want a solid brand. Everything you do in the marketing and selling of your product MUST be congruently aligned with the brand and its brand promise. Re-read that last sentence, it's vital you **get this!**

There is a price to pay if you want to associate with the popular kid, because his or her association alone makes you look better. People pay BIG BUCKS for these types of associations. Not everyone is going to be able to afford to associate with your brand. Re-read that last sentence again, too! If you want to be cool and want to own the name brand, you've got to pay a lot more than what the generic, common, ordinary, product costs—even though the product itself might be the same product. Is generic aspirin, any different than name brand aspirin? Baer Aspirin is different than Wal-Mart's version of Equate's aspirin. My spell checker won't even recognize 'Equate's' name in its database, but it recognizes the name brand Baer! Point made? I hope so.

But seriously!...they're the same product, only marketed under different brands. Why pay more? The answer is 'intrinsic value'.

Intrinsic value is the reason people will buy a $300,000 Rolls Royce Phantom, over a $100,000 BMW i7. They've been said to be built on the same chassis, have similar moving parts, but the Rolls Royce has three hundred percent the intrinsic value, because it's a Rolls Royce brand. People who have money would rather associate (generally speaking of course!) with owning a Rolls, because it has more built-in value and people believe it's a better car. The attributes between both cars is practically the same. The advantages are relatively similar; however, the Rolls brand has a different connotation than does a BMW. This connotation is associated with wealth and lifestyle of the wealthy, whereas BMW (though an expensive car in my opinion) has a different connotation—it's a car for working class executives who haven't necessarily 'made it' yet! It's more common, and there are more BMWs being bought than Rolls Royce's and for this 'scarcity' factor, the Rolls is more money! It's valued higher because of its brand reputation and promise. The promise is 'not everybody' or 'just anybody' can afford one. You have to more likely than not be wealthy and have boo-oodles of money to buy one.

As you develop your day launches keep these points in mind. Market accordingly; that is to say, stay true to your brand's promise, and have integrity about it. With this in mind, if you're selling a Rolls Royce information product, make sure it delivers on the brand promise that 'not anybody can afford it'. Make it exclusive, high priced, and cultivate a culture around the brand that people who buy it, judge it accordingly. Also, if you're selling a Rolls Royce-like information product, make sure it is of the highest quality out there.

Image is everything! Your product MUST represent its brand image to sell well, and in the future.

The next point I want to bring up is that I recommend that you create your marketing first. You do this by first developing the brand promise, i.e. slogan, and use the appropriate influence principles. If you don't know what these influence principles are I recommend you buy Robert Cialdini's book: INFLUENCE. You can pick-up a copy on Amazon. These principles are ones like reciprocity, scarcity, social proof, etc. You may find out about them by doing a simple Google Search.

Finally, the last point I want to mention to you about this Day Launch Formula approach is that it capitalizes on the fact that if you're an internet marketer with a well-developed e-mail list, that you can't always get everyone to buy what it is your marketing. For example, not everybody is going to be interested in creating their own launches. I get this! So not everybody on my e-mail list is going to buy this book! This formula capitalizes on this fact, because you'll be doing launches daily, unlike your competition, and so you are in a sense increasing your odds of selling products your list wants, because you have more products, on various subjects, that sometime they're bound to be interested in a particular launch product you roll out. Also, keep in mind that many people who are loyal to your products will want to BUY EVERYTHING you roll out. Food for thought!

SuperTinTin is going to record both your side of the video conversation as well as the person on the other side.

This is cool because you can literally create a training video with anyone, anywhere, and at any time that is convenient for both parties. This gives you a lot of flexibility and longitude whereas creating your day launch is concerned.

What I do is record one hour, and take a break, then go back and record part 2, which is another hour long video. I highly recommend you record two, two-hour-long videos. I say this because you'll be creating multiple income streams from these two hour-long videos. I'll talk more about that in a bit.

After you've finished the video tutorial on whatever you're teaching, thank your friend for their time, and ask for feedback on the training. Ask them what they like most about the training. Ask them what they liked least. Ask if everything you taught them made sense. And, ask how much they'd be willing to pay for a copy of the training videos? If they say nothing, ask it like this: "I'm sorry, I meant hypothetically, how much money do you think the training is worth, say if I were to sell it to other people who might be interested in the same topic?" You want to get their opinion and feedback, because this is going to help you get a better idea of how much 'practical value' your product has. Practical value is different from 'intrinsic' value. It is the measure of value irrespective of the brand. It's the value of the content alone. You want to make sure every product you release to the market has a lot of practical value. The last thing you ask your friend is to answer: (a) what are the attributes about this training you like best (explaining of course what attributes are), (b) off the top of your head what do you think the main advantages of each of these attributes is (have them do this without thinking about it), (c) what do you think for you personally the benefits of advantages would be, and (d) what common thread do you think runs through this particular training you and I did that best defines the experience? Also listen for hints about the values they elicit when they're giving you these answers. What you're doing, incidentally, if it wasn't already obvious, is determining the brand promise, so you have a sense of how to pitch the product in your integrated marketing messages throughout the various advertising channels you'll be utilizing. I always ask at the tail end of the conversation, just before parting ways, "If you had to use only one word to describe this training, what would it be?" I do this, because usually by this time they'll give you the most unconscious answer, which is the 'code breaker' that unlocks the secret to your brand. This is the 'reason' people will be buying your product, and what I typically will use (assuming I agree with their assessment) in my marketing messages to position and promote my day launch.

After you finish with them, take your video and upload it to Adobe's Premier Pro video editing suite. This is a fantastic video editing software, which will let you clean up your video, add intros and outros, and cut out the parts you don't want your buyers seeing. You can also copy-out the audio track, and save it as an MP3, which you need to do, because you'll be getting that over to a transcriptionist to transcribe next (but first things first). Once your video is edited, you'll want to go under the FILE menu, and export it, so you can RENDER the video into an MP4 format. Just save it in a directory on your hard-drive for now, where you'll be able to retrieve it shortly.

Okay, so the next step means jumping over to Fiverr.com, and hiring a transcriptionist to transcribe your audio tracks. Since each one is approximately an hour, it will likely cost you around ~$60 to have both hour-long audio tracks transcribed.

The transcriber is going to 'word-for-word' write out EXACTLY what's on the audio. After you get it back, you have two options: (a) you can edit and format the document yourself, or (b) you can hire someone else on Fiverr.com to edit it for you. They usually charge around $5 for every two-thousand words or so, but shop around. I also want to mention how it is a good idea to develop a strong relationship with a couple transcribers and editors, because you'll be using their services on a daily basis. So the more you use them, the more loyal they will be to you than to other occasional users of their services. In other words you're their bread-and-butter, and they will want to keep you happy, since you're helping them to pay their bills.

The next thing you need to do is hire another Fiverr.com 'gigster' to create an e-book cover for Kindle.

Simply search on the Fiverr Search box 'Kindle e-book covers' and you'll see many graphic artists offering this service for just $5. I want you to know upfront that most people have preferences about what they like, and think a book cover should look like, but you and the artist need to look past this limitation, and think about the brand-image, and brand-promise. You want a cover that reflects your brand; however, that being said, you also want a cover that sells your product on Amazon. Usually covers with stock photos of people on them sell better, but you also want to keep in mind the title of your book. The title should include likely terms, i.e. 'keywords' Amazon shoppers will be typing in the Amazon Search box to find products that are most closely related to what they're looking for. Your book must also have a 'subtitle' which should include more 'keywords' as well as a solution to the problem you're solving for the reader. Remember, and keep in the back of your mind, that the brand identity you create now, will follow this product throughout its entire lifecycle, so make sure you are truthful in your branding.

Now that you have the e-book finished completely, your videos edited, what you should be left with is a two hour long video course and Kindle e-book to sell. So what you want to do next is find a distribution channel for raking in profits from sales. Now that you have the files, you can use your Amazon S3 account you created and set-up to host, and make public your end product. So after you have your digital files hosted somewhere, you now need to concentrate on distribution channels. The first and most obvious is kdp.amazon.com where you'll immediately list your Kindle formatted book on your KDP account. You can alternatively list it using a specialized software program that is fairly inexpensive: kdpublishingpro.com. Once you have your Kindle e-book listed on Amazon's KDP platform, you've set your book up to begin selling on Amazon. This means as your book begins selling, you'll begin generating commissions from Amazon that can be direct deposited into your bank account. The next thing you can, and I would recommend doing is creating short three or four minute video talking about your launch book, and citing an Amazon link in the video's description area, where viewers can go and purchase your book. This will help promote the sale of your book, making more royalty income for you. The best part is once you set-it, you forget it. In other words, you no longer have to (unless you want to) promote your book, or do anything else with your book for that matter.

After you've setup your Kindle e-book, done your short YouTube video promoting it, it's time to take your launch to the next level. This means creating a 'sales page' and a 'thank-you page' on your own website/blog. The sales page will be what you promote through YouTube, social media sites, and even paid advertising (if you want to go that route). The thank-you page is where buyers will be taken after successfully purchasing your product. On this page you'll have download links where buyers can retrieve their purchase. As you build your launches up over time, you may even begin promoting other offers or offering discounts toward purchases of other day launch products you have created, for the 'sale-after-the-sale'. Often times when people have bought one thing, they're primed for buying something after the fact. This is a sales psychology principle many top sales professionals take advantage of, and I recommend you do also.

After you've setup you're your 'sales page' and 'thank-you page' you'll need to make a clone of each of these pages, either hosted on your existing website or some other site (I recommend Leadpages.net). These pages may have to be altered slightly to be approved by Click Bank's guidelines. Check with Click Bank on these requirements, by visiting their website: www.clickbank.com. You may also want to do a Google Search to get the information faster, and as of writing this book, I know there are YouTube videos that will walk you through the process of setting up your 'sales' and 'thank-you' pages to meet their requirements. Once this is accomplished the next thing to do is sell your product through Click Bank, which will help you sell the product through Click Bank's many affiliate marketers who are constantly and ever promoting new launch offers to their huge email lists. The more exposure to your product, the more sales opportunities; thus, the more money.

I found when I was first creating this system that a helpful tip was to take notes in EverNote about anything that might be the remotest bit confusing. If you do this, you'll have your notes to help you with subsequent future Day Formula Launches, so you save time and frustration.

Once your day launch is finished, and up on Click Bank, and your own self-hosted WordPress website, you can create another YouTube video promoting the entire launch in far greater detail. Make your video congruent with your brand, and insist that it has every bit as much value as what you're claiming it to have. Create success stories that you share on your videos and sales pages, give an extreme amount of value up-front; even before your buyer buys. Doing so will help you create enthusiasm for your product, and enhance the feelings of excitement when people stop to consider whether they need or want your product. Make your offers irresistible.

Lastly, after you've gone through this entire process, call it a day. Do something enjoyable, and entertaining—reason being—tomorrow you'll be doing this same exact process all over again.

I want to end this chapter by sharing why, even though this is a consistent process that you repeat each and every day, it never gets boring for me: I am constantly creating different products, learning new things around subjects that interest me, and have implemented this secret Day Launch Formula so many times that I can literally do my launches in a few hours now, and be able to enjoy the rest of my day. Also, I take the weekends off! ☺

Monetization Made Simple

Welcome to chapter 6, where we will be looking at some of the behind the scenes aspects of Day Launch Formula. So, I have designed this system as an accountability system, for those individuals who are hard-working, motivated, and willing to do whatever it takes to become wealthy from the Internet. I have never liked the idea of selling other people's products. There are too many other people doing exactly that. With Day Launch Formula—you create the product—you have other people sell it for you through the various affiliate channels, such as Click Bank.

So let's run some numbers here, shall we? There are 52 weeks in a year assuming that you work five days per week, creating one launch per day, you will have created 260 launches within the next 365 days. Now, I realize this seems like a lot of work, and it is, but keep in mind this system works for you, as much as you work for the results you want. This is why I call Day Launch Formula an accountability system. Even if you only work six months out of the year, five days per week, you'll still end up with 111 different launches you can roll out. For those of you even less motivated, and less thrilled about the prospect of working Monday through Friday rolling out launch after launch, even if you decide to work five months out of the year, that is a total of just 20 weeks, you will still create 100 new original launches. Namely, launches that you own all rights to, and which you control who sells your products and who does not, what the cost is, and all the terms (for the most part).

So let's just stick with round numbers here, and let's say that you have 100 launches per year—this is 100 products in your Day Launch portfolio. Each of these launches has a potential to make you boat-loads of money. You have dominated 100 different niches, simply by creating products people want to buy, and then positioning them as high-quality products inside unique niches with a marketplace full of consumers willing and wanting to buy more information about the things they care about. But, you also have 100 different Kindle e-books being sold online, through Kindle, all generating for you a ton of passive residual income month after month after month. This is in addition to the money that you're going to be making off of your personal launch pages (individual sales and thank you pages), which you have hosted on your WordPress website, in which you market and advertise yourself for.

Or, even the affiliate websites such as ClickBank.com; who are also selling your Day Launches through a vast arsenal of affiliate sellers (many who have immensely long lists of buyers) who are a huge percentage of your vast sales margins.

There are many ways to sell on the Internet. And of course I can't touch on all of those in this short book, but there are many other books available you can buy, courses that you can sit on, and independent research that you can do yourself (even launches you can develop around) in order to find out new and exciting ways of making money with the Day Launches you're constantly creating. This being said, you'll want to take stock of the fact that if you're constantly creating products, you're going to be somewhat busy and focused on the product development side of marketing, and for this reason you may want to enlist the help of freelancers, to help you market and sell your products as well. There are many creative ways of marketing and selling your launches that only require a little bit of thought.

You can even develop launches to teach other people some of these creative ideas that you have come up with. In fact this launch book that you're reading right now was actually developed around ideas that I had conceptualized and structured into this exact Day Launch Formula. Not only did I benefit from what is in my opinion an awesome and quick system for creating online wealth for yourself, but I also was able to take this exact system and market it to other people who wanted to do exactly the same so that they too could capitalize off of my ideas and insights. I want to say that it was Einstein who was quoted as saying, "The hardest thing for a man to do is think, and that is why so many people wind up doing mindless work." Don't quote me precisely on this quote, as I may have said it wrong, and I maybe even getting the person who quoted it wrong, but I've always liked this quote, because it rings true to what my experiences have been in dealing with other people. All it takes is a great idea and structuring it into a useable form, and you will have a steady supply of people willing and wanting to buy your product.

I love working from home. I've always found it so interesting that so many people could find creative ways of working from the comfort and convenience of their own residence, so as not to have to go to 9-to-5 job or work a wicked graveyard shift, and in doing so, come out more ahead in the course of a single year, than what most people will earn working in an average job. I think this is one reason I love the Day Launch Formula so much, because it helps people be able to do exactly this. It helps keep your brain in shape as well, because you're constantly coming up with new ideas to share with people, to help them improve processes and strategies for improving how they run their businesses and their personal lives. There are so many different things to learn about in life, and I am an avid reader, and have sat on so many courses that have cost me literally thousands upon thousands of dollars, that one day I just woke up and thought, "Why not do the same myself?" And so I have. And, let me share—I LOVE IT!

I cannot really rightly give you an estimate of how much money you can or might necessarily make. It will be up to you to discover all of this out on your own. I think a lot of it will depend on the specific niches you fill with your Day Launches, but also how you market and advertise your Day Launches. One thing, in my mind, that makes total sense, is that the more products you have, and the more residual assets you have, the more likely you are to make more money through passive residual means. The opportunities you create become your destiny later on.

There is definitely a sense of pride that comes when you've created your own product. It's exciting. It does something to you, which makes you feel as though you've accomplished something great. The best part is this feeling is very motivational. You can experience it every day, as you create more and more launches. The more launches you do, the easier this Day Launch Formula becomes, because you do it in your sleep, and more idea seem (in my opinion anyhow) to illuminate your mind.

Before I wrap up this chapter, I want to give you one more suggestion. This is more like a tip, and it's something I personally do, which I think just adds to the sales. There are now online plugins that work with WordPress which allow you to setup and sell online courses. What I do is take the same course, and edit it out over a series of modules, and create an online course to sell as well. This is easy to do, as you already have your content already. All you need to do is host the online course format and sell it on your blog, or other people's blogs. This creates a different flavor onto your product launch. It positions it more as an online course people can take. Different people feel and experience more value from having it structured this way. Others prefer just to download the content and get to work watching it offline in their convenience. I think giving people more options is a great way to make more money, by producing more sales opportunities. You can even hire a freelancer to create the courses for you, and even to upload them onto your WordPress site (just make sure you trust them to do a good job).

Please Read

This is fantastic. We have covered a lot of ground, in a very short period of time. I could have made this book hugely complex, going more in depth in other areas of marketing online, but I decided that less was actually best for most of you out there, because I knew you would take the information that I deliver to you, and make it your own process, following the exact formula that I have laid out for you in this book, and spread your wings and be able to fly independently.

When I first got started in Internet marketing, I didn't know the first thing about anything that I was doing. I just knew, somewhere in my heart of hearts, that I wanted to make a lot of money and do it entirely on the Internet.

You see... When I was in high school, the Internet was just moving into the realm where it was possible for peo-

ple to enter chat rooms and communicate with other people in different countries. When I was in elementary
school, we sent emails to pen pals in Japan, by writing
physical letters that were hand written, putting postage on
those letters, and then sending them off into the mail
(snail mail) in hopes that they would reach their final destination, and a letter would reach us back in return. In
those days Japan looked like another universe that was too
far for me to ever reach out to and communicate with. In
high school the paradigm changed, and the information
superhighway made it possible for human beings to connect with one another all entirely through this thing we
knew very little about called the Internet.

I remember when I started making connections with
people in foreign countries, like India, Japan, China, the
United Kingdom, Germany, and so many other countries.
It was fantastic, because we got to see a different side of
things that we had never known before. When you have
less information about something, it is easy to make blind
judgments and form opinions about things that you really
have no truthful clue about. I think this is one reason prej-
udice and racism and so many other problems that we've
had in our society has been out there in existence. Because,
we simply didn't have enough information, or enough insight, in order to be able to understand things as they truly
are in reality (I could debate reality for ever, too!).

This is the same thing with information that we are
delivering through our day launches. We want to dispel

myths as it relates to certain chunks of information that reside inside a small niche that only a select group of people, known as a *market place*, interact with one another and understand the culture of the market. Markets are interesting things. Markets are like small microcosmic universes; they can almost be thought of as many countries in a vast unknown world. I say this, because *every market*, and especially every niche market, at that, is different in some respects. It is unique in the sense that there is a language and culture that is common and usually only known to the individuals that do business and associate themselves in that marketplace. For example, in the hypnosis niche we use terminology, that people in other niches have no clue what the meaning is. It is unique and symbolic and representative of our particular niche. People outside of that niche, have a completely different understanding of what hypnosis is. They have a completely different understanding of what hypnosis is not. And our next-door neighbor the *pickup artists* who utilize hypnosis and neurolinguistic programming and other psychological and persuasion techniques to help them pickup dates—for the purpose of being with someone only one time—and then moving onto the next person to date. This neighbor of ours, i.e. the *pickup artist*, they have their own lingo, their own counterculture, and their own hotshots within that market—big fish in a little pond.

Where am I going with all of this? Where I am going is to uncharted territory, because it's now possible to do this. It is possible to do this because of the Internet, but

also too because of the Day Launch Formula that I've created and given over to you to use so that it might bring
great wealth into your own small microcosm reality.

The Day Launch Formula is a product that anybody
can use, though it's marketed specifically to Internet marketers in general and people who typically operate within
a small niche. The Day Launch Formula can help take you
from being a small fish in a small pond to being a big fish
in a small pond, very rapidly. The reason for this is, you
are simply creating more and more products for your
niche, as well as other niches—in order that you might
quickly climb from the bottom to the top almost instantly.
This is very, *very*, powerful, because you have to stop and
think for just a moment, to realize that most of the people
who are on the top of the ladder in most small niches, have
gotten there from writing books, doing training courses,
positioning themselves as experts and leaders, and from
having incredible marketing success through the Internet
and even traditional media outlets. Yet, you really need to
get it in your mind that the climb up that ladder for them
usually took a long, long, long, period of time. The journey was a long journey. Their journey had ups and downs,
and usually more downs. There were times along their
journey they probably wanted to give up. But not you.

That's right! Not you. No... You are special, your journey will be much faster, with less bumps in the road, and
your journey will take you from A to Z (or Zed), by by-

passing all the letters in between. You'll make your journey seem easy. And though it may not be easy, your journey will have a lot less hurdles to have to jump over than the other so-called experts who are dominating the niche that you currently want to be in and are passionate about toppling. And the main reason for this has to do with the fact that every single day from this point on albeit maybe you will take the weekends off, you will be creating product launch after product launch after product launch at such a rapid rate and speed, and in such a dynamic and moving way, that your competition simply will not be able to keep up. If they blink, they'll miss you passing them.

For many of the people who have already risen to the top inside the niche that you operate within, they are tired. These leaders or so-called leaders, they have made their journey and they found their destination, and now it's time for them to change that direction and chart a different course. For you, however, you are in a prime situation, because now you have at your disposal the knowledge that you need by engaging in and implementing the Day Launch Formula that you can literally jump above everyone in your way so that you can experience greatness and glory while making it look simple and easy.

We covered a lot of things in this book. Although the things we have covered may seem very simple, the truth of the matter is it isn't about how simple the steps are it actually is how precisely organized the formula is, and what the results have proven probabilistically. You will know your own statistics very soon, as you implement and roll out your new launches. For me, I operate within several niches, and I launch more products literally that I can even keep up with. These products bring in revenues that have created the type of lifestyle that always dreamt of having before implementing the Day Launch Formula. Our beta testers, these folks, they have taken our formula and without any prior experience or knowledge of the formula they've followed it precisely and for the most part have had wonderful results that have literally changed the way they do business. Many of the people who have beta tested our product; that is, the Day Launch Formula, these folks have quit their day jobs and have started working full time, entirely from their homes, doing exactly what it is we got lined up for you in this book.

My hope is that for you, whatever your goals are financially, whatever your goals are in your personal life, whatever you hope to achieve, and whatever success that you have in your mind needs to be attained to make you whole, my hope for you is that you get it sooner rather than later. I didn't write this book to make money, I didn't make this book to personify myself as some guru, because I really am not one. I'm just an individual who loves the solve problems, the more complex the problems the better, and I like to test things personally and then if they work allow other people to test them, until which time, I believe, that I've got something that is of the utmost value for people who want to work from home, and then I roll it out as quickly as humanely possible. I don't make any claims about the Day Launch Formula. Different people are going to have different results, and I know this, and you know this too. No two people are exactly the same. We are all different, and for that very reason alone you cannot predict with absolute certainty if someone is going to have success or someone is going to have failure. By success I simply mean that you make money with this thing called the Day Launch Formula. By failure I simply mean that you are going to lose money with this system. I have no clue. I make no promises.

We are all gifted with differences. I made mention in this book about the popular kid in high school, and how everyone wanted to be that popular kid. The popular kid is the one who had family money, they could buy the nice clothes. They were brought up in a confident household, with successful parents, who instilled these confidences to them, giving them an edge. They didn't want for much, and they didn't need much, all because of how they were pre-positioned and predispositioned in life. Not everybody is the popular kid. We have trends that pop up all the time in marketing. I remember when I was in middle school, it was slap bracelets that everyone wanted to own. Then what would you know, I think the company got sued because some kid accidentally slit their wrist and bled out, with one of the slap bracelets that had unraveled revealing the metal core of the product, or something like this. And in a blink of an instant the company was gone forever. I'm haven't seen or heard anyone make mention of slap brace-lets in probably over 15 years, probably longer. But I can still remember this trend and craze that everyone was so excited about. It was the cool thing. It was the hip thing. It was awesome, and everyone had to own it. And, the slap bracelet came about from the idea of one human being. It only takes one great idea in order to affect change all across the width and breadth of society. When something catches on it catches on like wildfire, and it spreads out of control into territories wide and far.

Perhaps in one of your launches you might be fortunate enough to have the same results as he got, i.e. the creator of the slap bracelet, I don't really know who created it, to be perfectly honest with you. But my point is you can create a product that people love, you can position it as the kid that is popular whom everybody wants to associate with and be. The kid that everyone wants to be and tries to imitate. And yet, at the end of the day we're all individuals. Every product that you create is going be different than the product your competitor is creating in some aspect and respect. For this reason, your marketing will be slightly different. Your sales will be slightly different. How you're perceived in the marketplace will be much different. It's about the flavor. Sometimes there are subtle differences in the flavor of a beverage, and sometimes there are staunch differences.

Growing up as a child we used to drink sweet tea and lemonade in the summertime. Sometimes a lemonade would taste fabulous, and sometimes the lemonade would suck, and not in the sour sense (no pun intended). Sometimes the sweet tea was sweet enough; just perfectly: not too sweet and yet not too unsweet. And then sometimes it was over sweetened or under sweetened. When you're developing your day launches I want you to think about this for a moment, because you want to position your product in the sweet spot everybody else will enjoy and criticize positively. You want to make it not too sweet and not too bitter. You want to add just enough wonderment to create a product that everybody wants to own and wants to share with other people. There are going to be some people that love *very sweet*, sweet tea. The problem with satisfying just the people who want *extremely sweet*, sweet tea is that you're going to be missing a lot of your market potential. And, as a result of making the tea too sweet, you will receive criticism from people who utterly denounce your tea calling it terrible and the worst they've ever had. And this will create a backlash that will actually lessen your opportunity to make sales. I don't want this for you. There is a middle ground, where everything is just good enough and it's a place that people are completely satisfied with, to the point where if it was any better they might complain and if it was any less they might complain. Your job is to make sure that your product gets to this place that I call middle ground, the best place to be.

The wonderful thing about the Day Launch Formula, is that you're free to research and experiment and to create whatever product you want. You are not restricted whatsoever, and you have the liberty of taking the things that you learn from researching, and creating one product, and being able to repurpose it into a future product sometime down the road. I do this all the time. And when I first got started doing day launches, I had no clue that this would be the reality. But there are things that I've learned as a result of doing day launches, constantly exercising my brain, and doing consistent research, that I've learned a great deal of information that I can now share with other people in different formats, and within different niche markets—and make money in the process.

When you're getting your product developed within a particular niche earlier we mentioned that you want to be in a niche that is not too specific and yet not too abstract. There's a lot of research that can go into finding more or less the sweet spot in a particular marketplace. When doing e-books for example you want to include keywords that are heavily researched yet write about topics where you have the opportunity to actually achieve a first-place ranking in a particular category representing a particular niche on Amazon.com. It takes research, it takes time, and it takes experience to learn how to do this. But, as you continue learning, and continue researching things for your day launches, you'll start to become cognizant and aware of all of the different things out there that you didn't know before that you can now use to enhance your next product launch and create an even more valuable product that people want to own.

My best advice, and concluding advice for you, is that you take your time with this, don't get too frustrated at first, and don't beat yourself up. The Day Launch Formula is meant for people to have fun with, continually being proving and improving themselves, while learning at the same time. The objective is that you solve problems for people in your marketplace, and present it in a way that has a potential to make you wealthy, while enlightening them.

In the olden days in India, and this is still true even today in India, young people would take a master which was called a 'guru' which is synonymous for 'teacher', and they would study with this individual, for years on end to learn the things that the master new. These wise sages would over time present information that they continued learning over their life so that the younger generation, i.e. there devout followers, would then be able to extend what they knew to future generations later on. This was the evolution of information, back then. And, today with the Internet, and all of the different databases that we have (academic databases, that is), we have so much to learn that we can learn it in such a short period of time, that had we been students of the guru back 5000 years ago in India, it would have taken us literally a lifetime and we still wouldn't know what we can learn in a single day today. Will we keep evolving information forward? I think so. I think information is there to help us solve some of the world's problems, and help other people learn things in ways that perhaps they couldn't always learn from other teachers and other products. So take pride in your day launch, and know that what you're doing is helping other people to master knowledge and information in a way that will help them improve their lives in some useful way. You are the change leaders of today, and I want you to know that when you do these day launches, you can take pride in knowing that not only are you learning, but you're helping other people to learn as well. The only difference between you and someone else teaching, is that you're always going to be the 'awesome teacher' who can present information in a way that students love learning. In a way, that is, that engages their learning, making them satisfied, intelligent, and wanting to always know more and more about a subject. Under no circumstances will you ever present information in your day launches like the 'boring teacher', because you know better. You understand that value comes before income. You understand that if you chase income; preferring it to value, that you'll likely remain broke for the remainder of your life. You understand that by always chasing value and wanting to help people, by creating more and more value, that they can appreciate and learn from, be engaged in, and themselves want to share their knowledge with other people in an excited fashion, that you will more likely than not— never want for anything—because you have the right mindset for creating abundant wealth for yourself. It always starts with value. Never does it start with chasing the almighty dollar. But, the money will come as a result; almost like it is some magical law of the universe.

I hope you've gotten a lot of value from this book. I enjoyed creating it for you. I literally wrote the entire thing, designed the book cover, and launched it up on Amazon, all in a single day's time. All on my own.

Now it's time for you to do the same!

Hastily yours,

Bryan Westra

Bibliography

Kern, Frank. (2014). *Convert*. Lajolla, California: Self Published.

Index

ABOUT THE AUTHOR

Bryan Westra is founder of Indirect Knowledge Limited
www.indirectknowledge.com

www.ingramcontent.com/pod-product-compliance
Lightning Source LLC
Chambersburg PA
CBHW051256050326
40689CB00007B/1217